Let's Read About Our Bodies/
Hablemos del cuerpo humano

Skin/La piel

By Cynthia Klingel and Robert B. Noyed

Reading consultant: Cecilia Minden-Cupp, Ph.D.,
Adjunct Professor, College of Continuing and Professional Studies, University of Virginia

Gareth Stevens
Publishing

Please visit our Web site www.garethstevens.com. For a free color catalog of all our high-quality books, call toll free 1-800-542-2595 or fax 1-877-542-2596.

Cataloging-in-Publication Data

Klingel, Cynthia.
  Skin / La piel by Cynthia Klingel and Robert B. Noyed.
    p. cm. — (Let's read about our bodies)
  Includes bibliographical references and index. Bilingual edition
  Summary: An introduction to skin, its uses, and how to take care of it.
  ISBN: 978-1-4339-3750-7 (lib. bdg.)
  ISBN: 978-1-4339-3751-4 (pbk.)
  ISBN: 978-1-4339-3752-1 (6-pack)
  1. Skin—Juvenile literature. [1. Skin. 2. Spanish-language materials] I. Noyed, Robert B. II. Title.

New edition published 2010 by
Gareth Stevens Publishing
111 East 14th Street, Suite 349
New York, NY 10003

New text and images this edition copyright © 2010 Gareth Stevens Publishing

Original edition published 2003 by Weekly Reader® Books
An imprint of Gareth Stevens Publishing
Original edition text and images copyright © 2003 Gareth Stevens Publishing

Art direction: Haley Harasymiw, Tammy Gruenewald
Page layout: Daniel Hosek, Katherine A. Goedheer
Editorial direction: Kerri O'Donnell, Diane Laska Swanke
Spanish translation: Eduardo Alamán

Photo credits: Cover © Image Source/Getty images; pp. 5, 9 Shutterstock.com; pp. 7, 11, 13, 15, 17, 19, 21 Gregg Andersen.

Printed in the United States of America

CPSIA compliance information: Batch #WW10GS: For further information contact Gareth Stevens, New York, New York at 1-800-542-2595.

Table of Contents

- -

Contenido

Boldface words appear in the glossary/
Las palabras en **negrita** aparecen en el glosario

Skin Is Special!

This is my skin.
It covers my body.

¡La piel es especial!

Esta es mi piel. La piel
cubre mi cuerpo.

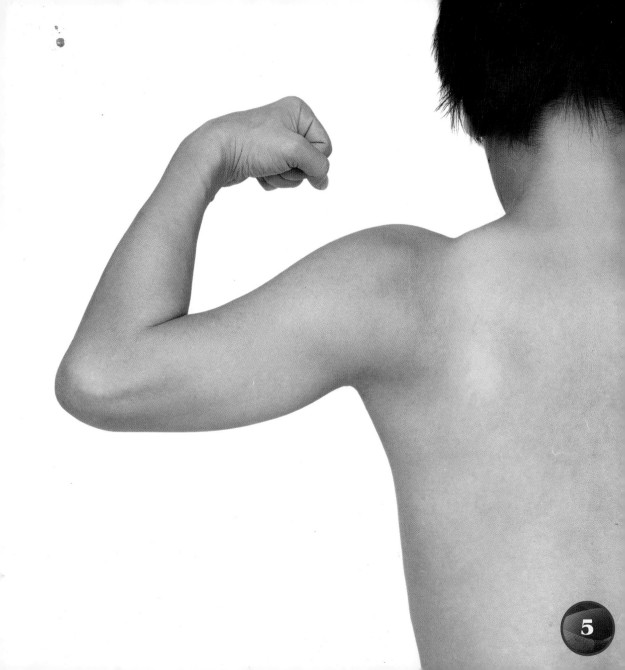

My skin helps keep me warm when it is cold.

Mi piel me ayuda a mantenerme caliente cuando hace frío.

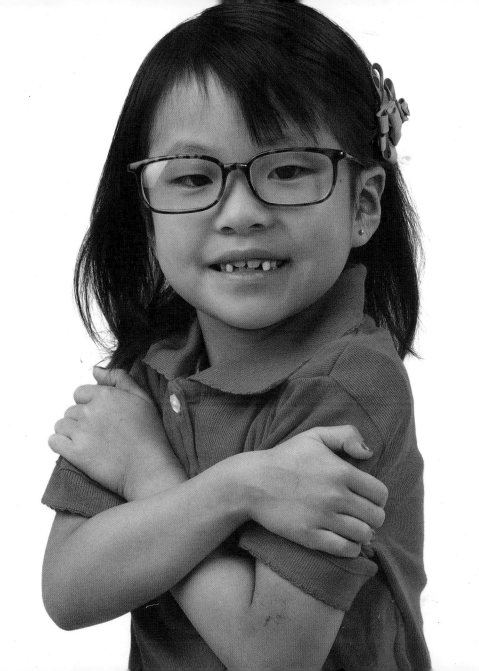

My skin helps keep me cool when it is hot.

Cuando hace calor, mi piel me ayuda a mantenerme fresca.

Skin comes in many colors.

La piel puede ser de muchos colores.

11

My skin has **freckles**.
Do you have freckles?

Mi piel tiene **pecas**.
¿Tú, tienes pecas?

13

Clean and Safe

I keep my skin clean. I wash my skin with soap and water.

Limpia y segura

Yo mantengo mi piel limpia. La lavo con agua y jabón.

15

Too much sun can burn my skin. I use **sunscreen** to keep my skin safe.

Demasiado sol puede quemarme la piel. Yo uso **bloqueador de sol** para mantener mi piel sana.

Sometimes I fall down and hurt my skin. My skin gets scraped.

A veces daño mi piel cuando me caigo. Me hago un raspón.

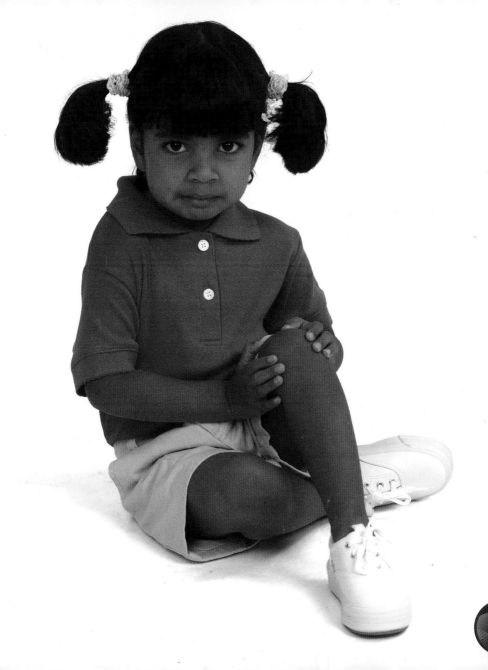

19

A **bandage** helps my skin **heal**.

El **vendaje** ayuda a que mi piel se **cure**.

Glossary/Glosario

bandage: a strip of cloth that covers a cut or scrape

freckles: small, brownish spots on the skin

heal: to make well

sunscreen: a lotion or cream that protects skin from the sun

- -

bloqueador de sol (el) Una loción o crema que protege la piel del sol

curar hacer sentir mejor

pecas (las) pequeños puntos marrones en la piel

vendaje (el) una tira de material suave que cubre raspones o heridas

For More Information/Más información

Books/Libros

DeGezelle, Terri. *Taking Care of My Skin*. Mankato, MN: Capstone Press, 2005.

Meachen Rau, Dana. La piel: *¿Qué hay dentro de mi?* Marshall Cavendish, 2006

Web Sites/Páginas de Internet

Why Does My Skin Get Wrinkly in Water?
kidshealth.org/kid/talk/qa/wrinkly_fingers.html
For information about how your skin works

Index/Índice

About the Authors

Cynthia Klingel has worked as a high school English teacher and an elementary school teacher. She is currently the curriculum director for a Minnesota school district. Cynthia Klingel lives with her family in Mankato, Minnesota.

Robert B. Noyed started his career as a newspaper reporter. Since then, he has worked in school communications and public relations at the state and national level. Robert B. Noyed lives with his family in Brooklyn Center, Minnesota.

- -

Información sobre los autores

Cynthia Klingel ha trabajado como maestra de secundaria y primaria. Cynthia es actualmente directora de planes de estudio en un distrito escolar en Minnesota. Cynthia Klingel vive con su familia en Mankato, Minnesota.

Robert B. Noyed comenzó su carrera como reportero. Desde entonces, ha trabajado en comunicación escolar y relaciones públicas a nivel estatal y nacional. Robert B. Noyed vive con su familia en Brooklyn Center, Minnesota.